MW01170170

Next-Gen Blending

Volume 2

Next-Gen Blending

Volume 2

50 More Easy & Delicious
BlendJet Recipes

Recipes & Photography
by Natalya Hardan

Published by

⊘ **blendjet**®

CONTENTS

INTRODUCTION

All great things deserve a sequel, so we're back at it again with 50 new mouthwatering recipes created specifically for the **BlendJet 2** portable blender. Whether you're into protein shakes, smoothies, or salad dressings, we've got you covered. These recipes aren't just ridiculously delicious, they're ridiculously easy to make. The only hard part is deciding which one to blend up first!

Happiness & healthiness are yours for the making,

— The BlendJet Creators

Ryan — John Kathryn Brian

PROUDLY VEGAN

These recipes feature plant-based ingredients, but you can substitute any milk or sweetener of your choice.

Let's face it, you threw away the instructions for your BlendJet 2 as soon as you took it out of the box. That's why we need to go over a few things before diving into these delectable recipes.

To get the most out of your BlendJet 2:

1.   Make sure the arrows on the rear of the jar are aligned to the arrows on the base.

2.   Always add liquid before solids. And don't overfill the jar!

3.   Screw the lid on snuggly before hitting the power button. A single press will give you a 20-second blend cycle. Hit it again to stop mid-cycle.

4.   Double-press the power button to activate Pulse Mode. You'll know it's active once the blue lights flash left to right three times and the swirl stays illuminated. Press and hold the power button repeatedly to pulse. Pulse Mode will automatically end after five seconds of inactivity.

5.   Recharge your BlendJet 2 with the included USB-C cable or use your own. You'll know it's fully charged when the light turns completely blue.

6.   And don't forget the best feature of all: BlendJet 2 cleans itself. Just add water, a drop of soap, and blend. We also recommend removing the gaskets periodically to do a deeper clean. See our how-to video at BlendJet.com/Guide.

CHAPTER 1
Groovy Smoothies

THEY'RE NUTRITIOUS
AND DELICIOUS

STRAWBERRY
CHEESECAKE
Smoothie

Ingredients

milk of choice	1 cup
yogurt of choice	¼ cup
graham cracker crumbs	2 Tbsp
cream cheese of choice	1 Tbsp
agave or sweetener of choice	1 Tbsp
vanilla extract	½ tsp
frozen strawberries, float to top	

Directions

Add all ingredients to the BlendJet and
blend for 2 cycles. Enjoy!

TOTAL TIME
5 MIN.

SERVINGS
1

STRESS BUSTER ORANGE
Smoothie

Ingredients

orange juice	½ cup
milk of choice	½ cup
small orange, peeled	1
frozen banana	½
carrots, peeled and sliced	¼ cup
vanilla extract	½ tsp

Directions

Add all ingredients to the BlendJet and
blend for 2-3 cycles. Enjoy!

TOTAL TIME   **SERVINGS**

5 MIN.   **1**

LEMON
PINEAPPLE
Smoothie

Ingredients

. . . .

milk of choice   ¾ cup
lemon juice   ¼ cup
yogurt of choice   ¼ cup
frozen pineapple   ½ cup
frozen banana   ½
ice, float to top

Directions

. . . .

Add all ingredients to the BlendJet and
blend for 1-2 cycles. Enjoy!

TOTAL TIME   SERVINGS
5 MIN.   **1**

14

CREAMY KALE
COCONUT KIWI
Smoothie

Ingredients

coconut milk	½ cup
coconut water	½ cup
kale	½ cup
frozen banana	½
kiwi	½
coconut flakes	1 Tbsp
ice, float to top	

Directions

Add all ingredients to the BlendJet and
blend for 2-4 cycles. Enjoy!

TOTAL TIME   SERVINGS
5 MIN.   **1**

RASPBERRY LIME
Smoothie

Ingredients

milk of choice	1 cup
frozen raspberries	1 cup
yogurt of choice	½ cup
agave or sweetener of choice	1 Tbsp
juice of 1 small lime	
zest of 1 small lime	

Directions

Add all ingredients to the BlendJet and
blend for 1 cycle. Enjoy!

TOTAL TIME
5 MIN.

SERVINGS
1

BLACK FOREST
Smoothie

Ingredients

milk of choice	1 cup
frozen cherries	1 cup
yogurt of choice	¼ cup
cocoa powder	1 Tbsp
agave or sweetener of choice	1 Tbsp
vanilla extract	¼ tsp

Directions

Add all ingredients to the BlendJet and
blend for 1-2 cycles. Enjoy!

TOTAL TIME   SERVINGS

5 MIN.   **1**

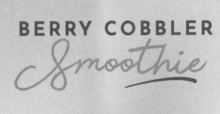

BERRY COBBLER
Smoothie

Ingredients

milk of choice	1 cup
mixed frozen berries	1 cup
yogurt of choice	¼ cup
granola	¼ cup
maple syrup or sweetener of choice	1 Tbsp
vanilla extract	¼ tsp
cinnamon	¼ tsp
ice, float to top	

Directions

Add all ingredients to the BlendJet and
blend for 2-4 cycles. Top with granola and
enjoy!

TOTAL TIME   **SERVINGS**

5 MIN.   **1**

IMMUNITY
BOOSTING
Smoothie

Ingredients

orange juice	1 cup
frozen banana	½
frozen mango	¼ cup
chia seeds	1 tsp
grated ginger	½ tsp
cinnamon	¼ tsp
turmeric	¼ tsp
ice, float to top	

Directions

Add all ingredients to the BlendJet and
blend for 1-2 cycles. Enjoy!

TOTAL TIME   SERVINGS
5 MIN.   **1**

XL JAR
BANANA BREAD
Smoothie

Ingredients

milk of choice	2 cups
frozen banana	1
granola of choice	¾ cup
yogurt of choice	½ cup
vanilla extract	½ tsp
cinnamon	¼ tsp
pinch of ground nutmeg	
ice, float to top	

Directions

Add all ingredients to the BlendJet XL 32 oz Jar and **blend for 1-2 cycles.** If using the included 16 oz BlendJet jar instead of the XL jar, cut the recipe in half. Dust with a little cinnamon and enjoy!

TOTAL TIME
5 MIN.

SERVINGS
2

WHITE CHOCOLATE
RASPBERRY
Smoothie

Ingredients

milk of choice	1 cup
frozen raspberries	1 cup
yogurt of choice	¼ cup
white chocolate chips	2 Tbsp

Directions

Add all ingredients to the BlendJet and
blend for 2-3 cycles. Enjoy!

TOTAL TIME
5 MIN.

SERVINGS
1

CHAPTER 2
Protein Power
FEEL-GOOD FUEL

VANILLA MATCHA
Protein Shake

Ingredients

milk of choice	1 cup
agave or sweetener of choice	1 Tbsp
small handful spinach	1
scoop vanilla protein powder	1
matcha powder	1 tsp
ice, float to top	

Directions

Add all ingredients to the BlendJet and
blend for 1-2 cycles. Enjoy!

TOTAL TIME
5 MIN.

SERVINGS
1

CAKE BATTER

Protein Shake

Ingredients

milk of choice	1 cup
frozen banana	½
cashew or nut butter of choice	1 Tbsp
vanilla protein powder	1 scoop
vanilla extract	½ tsp
ice, float to top	

Directions

Add all ingredients to the BlendJet and
blend for 1 cycle. Enjoy!

TOTAL TIME   SERVINGS
5 MIN.   **1**

PEACH MANGO
Protein Shake

Ingredients

milk of choice	1 cup
frozen peaches	½ cup
frozen mangos	½ cup
vanilla protein powder	1 scoop

Directions

Add all ingredients to the BlendJet and
blend for 2-3 cycles. Enjoy!

TOTAL TIME
5 MIN.

SERVINGS
1

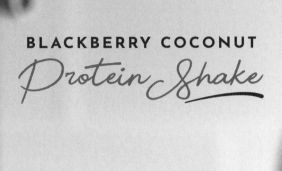

BLACKBERRY COCONUT
Protein Shake

Ingredients

coconut milk	1 cup
frozen blackberries	½ cup
frozen banana	½
coconut flakes	1 Tbsp
vanilla protein powder	1 scoop
ice, float to top	

Directions

Add all ingredients to the BlendJet and
blend for 2-4 cycles. Enjoy!

TOTAL TIME
5 MIN.

SERVINGS
1

TROPICAL PUNCH
Protein Shake

Ingredients

coconut milk	1 cup
frozen mango chunks	½ cup
frozen pineapple chunks	½ cup
frozen banana	½
vanilla protein powder	1 scoop

Directions

Add all ingredients to the BlendJet and
blend for 1-2 cycles. Enjoy!

TOTAL TIME
5 MIN.

SERVINGS
1

MINT CHOCOLATE CHIP
Protein Shake

Ingredients

milk of choice	1 cup
yogurt of choice	¼ cup
small handful baby spinach	
chocolate protein powder	1 scoop
maple syrup or sweetener of choice	1 Tbsp
peppermint extract	¼ tsp
ice, float to top	

Directions

Add all ingredients to the BlendJet and
blend for 1 cycle. Enjoy!

TOTAL TIME
5 MIN.

SERVINGS
1

STRAWBERRY
PEANUT BUTTER
Protein Shake

Ingredients

milk of choice	1 cup
frozen strawberries	1 cup
banana	½
peanut butter	2 Tbsp
vanilla protein powder	1 scoop

Directions

Add all ingredients to the BlendJet and
blend for 1-2 cycles. Enjoy!

TOTAL TIME
5 MIN.

SERVINGS
1

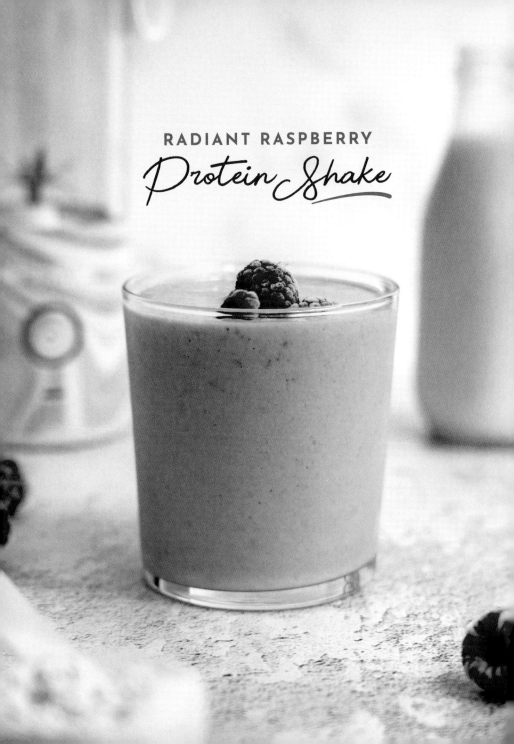

RADIANT RASPBERRY
Protein Shake

Ingredients

milk of choice	1 cup
frozen raspberries	1 cup
frozen banana	½
vanilla protein	1 scoop

Directions

Add all ingredients to the BlendJet and
blend for 1-2 cycles. Top with frozen
raspberries, and **enjoy!**

TOTAL TIME
5 MIN.

SERVINGS
1

RED VELVET CAKE
Protein Shake

Ingredients

milk of choice	1 cup
frozen banana	½
chocolate protein powder	1 scoop
maple syrup or sweetener of choice	1 Tbsp
beet powder	1 tsp
ice, float to top	

Directions

Add all ingredients to the BlendJet and
blend for 1 cycle. Top with chocolate pieces or
cacao nibs and **enjoy!**

TOTAL TIME	SERVINGS
5 MIN.	**1**

TIRAMISU
Protein Shake

Ingredients

milk of choice	½ cup
chilled coffee	½ cup
vanilla protein powder	1 scoop
yogurt of choice	2 Tbsp
cocoa powder	1 tsp
ice, float to top	

Directions

Add all ingredients to the BlendJet and **blend for 1 cycle.** Top with chocolate pieces or cacao nibs and **enjoy!**

TOTAL TIME
5 MIN.

SERVINGS
1

CHAPTER 3
Café BlendJet
BRING THE COFFEE SHOP WITH YOU

JAVA CHIP *frappé*

Ingredients

milk of choice	½ cup
espresso	2 oz (¼ cup)
melted chocolate	1 Tbsp
maple syrup or sweetener of choice	1 Tbsp
cocoa powder	1 Tbsp
ice, float to top	

Directions

Add all ingredients to the BlendJet and **blend for 2 cycles.** Top with your whipped cream of choice and a drizzle of melted chocolate. **Enjoy!**

TOTAL TIME
5 MIN.

SERVINGS
1

HONEY
LAVANDER
frappé

Ingredients

milk of choice	½ cup
espresso	2 oz (¼ cup)
lavender simple syrup	1 Tbsp
honey	1 Tbsp
ice, float to top	

Directions

Add all ingredients to the BlendJet and
blend for 1 cycle. Top with your whipped cream of
choice and a drizzle of honey. **Enjoy!**

TOTAL TIME   SERVINGS
5 MIN.   **1**

PEPPERMINT
mocha frappé

Ingredients

milk of choice	1 cup
espresso	2 oz (¼ cup)
melted chocolate	2 Tbsp
cocoa powder	1 Tbsp
peppermint extract	½ tsp
ice, float to top	

Directions

Add all ingredients to the BlendJet and
blend for 1 cycle. Top with your whipped cream of
choice and dark chocolate shavings. **Enjoy!**

TOTAL TIME
5 MIN.

SERVINGS
1

MATCHA *frappé*

Ingredients

milk of choice	1 cup
maple syrup or sweetener of choice	1 Tbsp
matcha powder	2 tsp
vanilla extract	½ tsp
ice, float to top	

Directions

Add all ingredients to the BlendJet and
blend for 1-2 cycles. Top with your whipped
cream of choice and a dust of matcha powder.
Enjoy!

TOTAL TIME
5 MIN.

SERVINGS
1

CINNAMON
DOLCE
latte

Ingredients

milk of choice	½ cup
chilled coffee	½ cup
maple syrup or sweetener of choice	1 Tbsp
cinnamon powder	1 tsp
vanilla extract	½ tsp
ice, float to top	

Directions

Add all ingredients to the BlendJet and
blend for 1-2 cycles. Top with your whipped
cream of choice and a dust of cinnamon.
Enjoy!

TOTAL TIME   SERVINGS
5 MIN.   **1**

HAZELNUT
CARAMEL
mocha

Ingredients

milk of choice	1 cup
espresso	2 oz (¼ cup)
cocoa powder	1 Tbsp
caramel	1 Tbsp
hazelnut extract	½ tsp
ice, float to top	

Directions

Add all ingredients to the BlendJet and
blend for 1 cycle. Top with your whipped cream
of choice, a dust of cocoa powder and a drizzle of
caramel. **Enjoy!**

TOTAL TIME
5 MIN.

SERVINGS
1

SALTED CARAMEL
mocha frappé

Ingredients

chocolate milk of choice   ½ cup
espresso   2 oz (¼ cup)
caramel   2 Tbsp
pinch of salt
ice, float to top

Directions

Add all ingredients to the BlendJet and
blend for 2 cycles. Top with your whipped cream of
choice and a drizzle of caramel. **Enjoy!**

TOTAL TIME   **SERVINGS**
5 MIN.   **1**

CHAPTER 4

Cocktails, anyone?

IT'S 5 O'CLOCK
SOMEWHERE

STRAWBERRIES
& CREAM
Mudslide

Ingredients

Cream Layer

Kahlua	1 oz
vodka	2 oz
vanilla ice cream	2 scoops

Strawberry Layer

coffee creamer of choice	2 oz
strawberries, halved	5

Directions

Add Kahlua, vodka, and vanilla ice cream to the BlendJet and **blend for 1 cycle.** Pour into a glass and set aside. Clean out the BlendJet. Add coffee creamer and strawberries to the BlendJet and **blend for 1 cycle.** Pour strawberry mixture on top of the cream mixture and **enjoy!**

TOTAL TIME
10 MIN.

SERVINGS
1-2

FROZEN IRISH
Coffee

Ingredients

Irish Whiskey	1.5 oz
Bailey's Irish Cream	1 oz
Kahlua	1 oz
espresso	1.5 oz
vanilla ice cream	2 scoops
ice, float to top	

Directions

Add all ingredients to the BlendJet and **blend for 1-2 cycles.** Top with your whipped cream of choice (optional) and crushed coffee beans. **Enjoy!**

TOTAL TIME
5 MIN.

SERVINGS
1

JALAPEÑO MEZCAL
Margarita

Ingredients

. . . .

triple sec	2 oz
mezcal	1 oz
lime juice	¼ cup
agave	2 Tbsp
jalapeño peppers	2 Tbsp
ice, float to top	

Directions

. . . .

Add all ingredients to the BlendJet and
blend for 1-2 cycles. Enjoy!

TOTAL TIME
5 MIN.

SERVINGS
1

FROZEN COCONUT

Mojito

Ingredients

coconut water	¼ cup
full-fat coconut milk	¼ cup
rum	2 oz
lime juice	¼ cup
agave	2 Tbsp
mint leaves	Approx. 15
ice, float to top	

Directions

Add all ingredients to the BlendJet, and
blend for 2-3 cycles. Enjoy!

TOTAL TIME
5 MIN.

SERVINGS
1

PINEAPPLE
Daiquiri

Ingredients

white rum	2 oz
lime juice	2 Tbsp
agave or sweetener of choice	2 Tbsp
frozen pineapple chunks, float to top	

Directions

Add all ingredients to the BlendJet, and
blend for 1-2 cycles. Enjoy!

TOTAL TIME   **SERVINGS**

5 MIN.   **1**

XL JAR
SPIKED COCONUT
Limeade

Ingredients

silver tequila	4 oz
lime juice	¼ cup
coconut milk	½ cup
agave or sweetener of choice	3 Tbsp
ice	3 cups

Directions

Add all ingredients to the BlendJet XL 32 oz Jar and **blend for 2 cycles.** If using the included 16 oz BlendJet jar instead of the XL jar, cut the recipe in half. **Enjoy!**

TOTAL TIME
5 MIN.

SERVINGS
1

FROZEN STRAWBERRY *Margarita*

Ingredients

triple sec	1.5 oz
tequila	1 oz
lime juice	¼ cup
agave or sweetener of choice	2 Tbsp
frozen strawberries	1 cup
ice, float to top	

Directions

Add all ingredients to the BlendJet, and
blend for 2-3 cycles. Enjoy!

TOTAL TIME
5 MIN.

SERVINGS
1

WATERMELON VODKA
Slushie

Ingredients

vodka	2 oz
agave or sweetener of choice	2 Tbsp
juice of 1 lime	
watermelon chunks	1 cup
ice, float to top	

Directions

Add all ingredients to the BlendJet, and
blend for 1-2 cycles. Enjoy!

TOTAL TIME
5 MIN.

SERVINGS
1

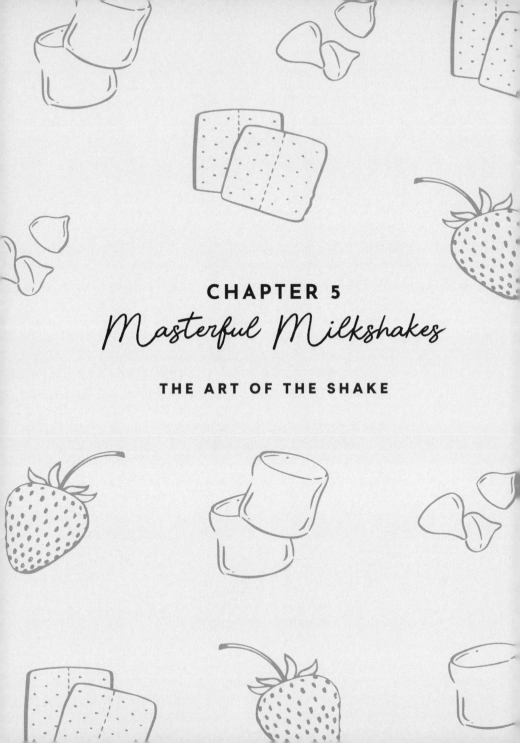

CHAPTER 5

Masterful Milkshakes

THE ART OF THE SHAKE

PUMPKIN
CHEESECAKE
Milkshake

Ingredients

milk of choice	1 cup
pumpkin puree	½ cup
cream cheese of choice	1 Tbsp
graham cracker crumbs	1 Tbsp
pumpkin pie spice	½ tsp
vanilla ice cream of choice, float to top	

Directions

Add all ingredients to the BlendJet and **blend for 1 cycle.** Top with your whipped cream of choice and a sprinkle of graham cracker crumbs. **Enjoy!**

TOTAL TIME
5 MIN.

SERVINGS
1

WHITE CHOCOLATE RASPBERRY
Milkshake

Ingredients

milk of choice	¾ cup
frozen raspberries	1 cup
melted white chocolate	2 Tbsp
vanilla ice cream of choice, float to top	

Directions

Add all ingredients to the BlendJet and **blend for 1 cycle.** Top with your whipped cream of choice. **Enjoy!**

TOTAL TIME
5 MIN.

SERVINGS
1

STRAWBERRY MARSHMALLOW *Milkshake*

Ingredients

milk of choice	¾ cup
frozen strawberries	1 cup
marshmallow fluff	2 Tbsp
vanilla ice cream of choice, float to top	

Directions

Add all ingredients to the BlendJet and **blend for 1 cycle.** Top with your whipped cream of choice. **Enjoy!**

TOTAL TIME
5 MIN.

SERVINGS
1

KEY LIME PIE
Milkshake

Ingredients

milk of choice	¾ cup
key lime juice	¼ cup
graham cracker crumbs	2 Tbsp
lime zest	½ tsp
vanilla ice cream, float to top	

Directions

Add all ingredients to the BlendJet and **blend for 1 cycle.** Top with your whipped cream of choice and graham cracker crumbs. **Enjoy!**

TOTAL TIME
5 MIN.

SERVINGS
1

ROCKY ROAD
CHOCOLATE
Milkshake

Ingredients

chocolate milk of choice	1 cup
mini marshmallows	¼ cup
sliced almonds	1 Tbsp
Rocky Road ice cream, float to top	

Directions

Add all ingredients to the BlendJet and **blend for 1-2 cycles.** Top with mini marshmallows and your chocolate syrup of choice. **Enjoy!**

TOTAL TIME
5 MIN.

SERVINGS
1

CARAMEL APPLE
Milkshake

Ingredients

apple juice   1 cup
caramel sauce   2 Tbsp
vanilla ice cream of choice, float to top

Directions

Add all ingredients to the BlendJet and
blend for 1-2 cycles. Top with your whipped
cream of choice and a drizzle of caramel.
Enjoy!

TOTAL TIME   **SERVINGS**
5 MIN.   **1**

CRÈME BRÛLÉE
Milkshake

Ingredients

milk of choice   1 cup
caramel   2 Tbsp
vanilla ice cream of choice, float to top

Directions

Add all ingredients to the BlendJet and
blend for 1-2 cycles. Top with your whipped
cream of choice and a drizzle of caramel.
Enjoy!

TOTAL TIME   **SERVINGS**
5 MIN.   **1**

CHAPTER 6
Delicious Dips
& Dressings

DITCH THE STORE-BOUGHT STUFF

RASPBERRY
Vinaigrette

Ingredients

olive oil	½ cup
red wine vinegar	¼ cup
raspberries	1 cup
diced onion	2 Tbsp
Dijon mustard	1 tsp
salt	¼ tsp
black pepper	1 pinch

Directions

Add all ingredients to the BlendJet and **blend for 2-3 cycles.** Pour over your salad of choice and **enjoy!**

TOTAL TIME
5-10 MIN.

SERVINGS
Makes about 1 cup of dressing

GREEN GODDESS
Hummus

Ingredients

lemon juice	6 Tbsp
tahini	¼ cup
olive oil	2 Tbsp
parsley	½ cup
basil	¼ cup
chives	2 Tbsp
garlic clove	1
salt	½ tsp
chickpeas	1 can

Directions

Add all ingredients except chickpeas to the BlendJet and **blend for 1 cycle.** Add the chickpeas and **blend again for 3-5 cycles,** or until desired consistency is achieved. If at any point it becomes difficult to blend, add a little lemon juice or tahini and **continue blending.** Serve with pita bread and **enjoy!**

TOTAL TIME
15 MIN.

SERVINGS
Serves 3-4

EASY BLENDER
Salsa

Ingredients

fire-roasted tomatoes	½ can
small onion, chopped	½
jalapeño, chopped with seeds removed	½ - 1
garlic, chopped	1 clove
cilantro	½ cup
juice of 1 lime	
salt	½ tsp
cumin	½ tsp
chili powder	½ tsp

Directions

Add all ingredients to the BlendJet and **blend for 1-2 cycles** (1 cycle for a chunkier salsa or 2 cycles for a smoother salsa). Serve with tortilla chips and **enjoy!**

TOTAL TIME
10 MIN.

SERVINGS
Serves 3-4

THOUSAND ISLAND
Dressing

Ingredients

mayonnaise of choice	1 cup
ketchup	½ cup
dill pickle relish	2 Tbsp
onion, diced	2 Tbsp
lemon juice	1 Tbsp
salt	½ tsp
black pepper	¼ tsp

Directions

Add all ingredients to the BlendJet and **blend for 2 cycles.** Pour over your salad of choice and **enjoy!**

TOTAL TIME
5-10 MIN.

SERVINGS
Makes a little over 1 cup of dressing

STRAWBERRY
BALSAMIC
Vinaigrette

Ingredients

olive oil	2 Tbsp
apple cider vinegar	2 Tbsp
honey or sweetener of choice	2 Tbsp
poppy seeds	1 Tbsp
strawberries, halved	1 cup
salt	¼ tsp
black pepper	⅛ tsp

Directions

Add all ingredients to the BlendJet and
blend for 1 cycle. Pour over your salad of
choice and **enjoy!**

TOTAL TIME

5-10 MIN.

SERVINGS

Makes
about 1 cup
of dressing

CITRUS
Vinaigrette

Ingredients

olive oil	½ cup
juice of 1 large orange	
juice of 1 lemon	
juice of 1 lime	
zest of 1 lemon	
apple cider vinegar	1 Tbsp
agave	1 Tbsp
Dijon mustard	1 Tbsp
salt	¼ tsp
cayenne pepper	⅛ tsp

Directions

Add all ingredients to the BlendJet and
blend for 1 cycle. Pour over your salad of
choice and **enjoy!**

TOTAL TIME

10 MIN.

SERVINGS
Makes
about 1 cup
of dressing

XL JAR
SUN-DRIED TOMATO
Pasta Sauce

Ingredients

milk of choice	2 cups
creamer of choice	¼ cup
yogurt of choice	¼ cup
sun-dried tomatoes	¾ cup
basil leaves	½ cup
parmesan cheese of choice	¼ cup
tomato paste	1 Tbsp
garlic	2 cloves
onion powder	½ tsp
salt	½ tsp
black pepper	¼ tsp

Directions

Add all ingredients to the BlendJet XL 32 oz Jar and **blend for 2-3 cycles**. If using the included 16 oz BlendJet jar instead of the XL jar, cut the recipe in half. Pour over your pasta of choice, then garnish with more sun-dried tomatoes and finely chopped basil. **Enjoy!**

TOTAL TIME
15 MIN.

SERVINGS
Makes about
3 cups of
pasta sauce

MAPLE DIJON
Dressing

Ingredients

milk of choice	2 cups
olive oil	½ cup
apple cider vinegar	¼ cup
maple syrup	2 Tbsp
Dijon mustard	1 Tbsp
garlic	1 clove
salt	1 pinch
black pepper	1 pinch

Directions

Add all ingredients to the BlendJet and **blend for 1 cycle.** Pour over your salad of choice and **enjoy!**

TOTAL TIME

5-10 MIN.

SERVINGS

Makes about 1 cup of dressing

About the Author

Meet BlendJet's official recipe creator **Natalya Hardan**—founder of Healthiir, a platform dedicated to making plant-based eating easy! Her blended recipes require little time and use only the best ingredients. Together, we're on a mission to make consuming real, whole foods simple, delicious and rewarding.

Visit *blendjet.com/recipes* for our complete recipe collection.

Join our BlendJet Recipes Facebook Group to share your creations and discover fan-made favorites.

Follow us **@blendjet** for a fresh new recipe each week.